GW00336269

First published in Great Britain in 1996 by Brockhampton Press,
a member of the Hodder Headline Group,
20 Bloomsbury Street, London WC1B 3QA.

This series of Little Gift books was made by Frances Banfield,
Kate Brown, Laurel Clark, Penny Clarke, Clive Collins, Melanie
Cumming, Nick Diggory, Deborah Gill, David Goodman, Douglas
Hall, Maureen Hill, Nick Hutchison, John Hybert, Kate Hybert,
Douglas Ingram, Simon London, Patrick McCreeth, Morse Modaberi,
Tara Neill, Anne Newman, Grant Oliver, Michelle Rogers,
Nigel Soper, Karen Sullivan and Nick Wells.

Compilation and selection copyright
© 1996 Brockhampton Press.

ISBN 1 86019 465 6
A copy of the CIP data is available from the
British Library upon request.

Produced for Brockhampton Press by Flame Tree Publishing,
a part of The Foundry Creative Media Company Limited,
The Long House, Antrobus Road, Chiswick W4 5HY.

Printed and bound in Italy by L.E.G.O. Spa.

The Funny Book of
FATHERS

Words selected by
Bob Hale

Cartoons by
Dicky Howett

BROCKHAMPTON
PRESS

*Back in a moment Simon – I'm sure you
and daddy have lots to talk about...*

She comes from a tennis-playing family.
Her father's a dentist.
BBC tennis commentator

Victor Emmanuel II of Italy (1820-1878) was
popularly known as the Father of his Country,
in allusion to his unnumbered progeny
of bastard children.

The poet Robert Graves, in the 1920s,
found himself acquiring the 'faculty of working
through constant interruptions ... recognising the
principal varieties of babies' screams - hunger,
indigestion, wetness, pains, boredom, wanting
to be played with.'

Father's Day is the day to remember
the forgotten man.

Anonymous

A father now who sees his infant born,
What joy, oh, what delight! At once he wraps
The babe in napkins and in swaddling-clothes;
And like a pair of scales he loads him up
And hangs about the neck a thousand things -
Wolves' teeth and figs, half-moons and coral too,
Toy pigs and badgers, till the infant looks
Just like the man who hawks around old clothes.
He hires a nurse and prattles baby talk,
And has no eye for any other thing,
'How is my little love, my little pet?
Your papa loves you well, you are his joy,
Your mamma's only treasure,' there he sits
List'ning amazed to 'cacca' and 'pappa'.
While in his lap, the baby wets him through.

Giambattista Basile, **The Pentamerone**

Need a hand with the kite, dad..?

Don't fret dear, I'm just giving the baby his bottle...

Mr Palmer maintained the common, but unfatherly, opinion among his sex, of all infants being alike; and although he could plainly perceive at different times, the most striking resemblance between this baby and everyone of his relations on both sides, there was no convincing his father of it; no persuading him to believe that it was not exactly like every other baby of the same age; nor could he even be brought to acknowledge the simple proposition of its being the finest child in the world.

*Jane Austen, **Sense and Sensibility***

'Lullaby, oh, lullaby!'
Thus I heard a father cry
'Lullaby, oh, lullaby!
The brat will never shut an eye;
Hither come, some power divine!
Close his lids or open mine!'

*Thomas Hood, **A Serenade***

How many sons inherit their
Fathers Failings, as well as Estates?

Fourteenth century

When Sheridan's School for Scandal came out,
Richard Cumberland's children prevailed upon
their father to take them to see it - they had
the stage box - their father was seated behind
them; and as the story was told by a friend of
Sheridan's, who was close by, every time the
children laughed at what was going on the
stage, he pinched them, and said, 'What are
you laughing at, my dear little folks? You
should not laugh, my angels; there is nothing
to laugh at' - and then, in an undertone,
'Keep still, you little dunces.'

Have you thought of a name for the baby yet, dear..?

He's getting a big boy now isn't he Mr Connolly..?

My father's literary industry was prodigious.
'I never knew such a reader,' said my mother.
'When the conductor gives him his ticket in
the tram, he turns it over and reads the back.'

Guy Boas

Simon had been warned that he must be on
his best behaviour when his wealthy aunt
arrived for a brief holiday visit. It was at tea
during the first day of her stay that Simon kept
looking at his aunt; then, when the meal was
almost finished, he asked: 'Auntie, when are
you going to do your trick?'
'What trick is that, dear?' she enquired.
'Well,' began Simon, 'Daddy says
you can drink like a fish.'

The Huge Joke Book

Walter de la Mare (1873-1956) lay for three
weeks at the very gates of death. On one of
these days his younger daughter said to him
as she left him, 'Is there nothing I could get
for you - fruit or flowers?' In a weak voice he
replied, 'No, no, my dear; too late for fruit,
too soon for flowers!'

D.H. Lawrence told of how his father struggled
through half a page of *The White Peacock* 'and it
might as well have been Hottentot. "And what
dun they gie thee for that, lad?" "Fifty pounds,
father." "Fifty pounds!" He was dumbfounded,
and looked at me with shrewd eyes, as if I were
a swindler. "Fifty pounds! An' tha's niver
done a day's hard work in thy life."

You could at least remember their names!

My dad's big isn't he...

... the poorest poor
Long for some moments in a weary life
When they can know and feel that they have been
Themselves the fathers and the dealers out
Of some small blessings.
Wordsworth, **The Old Cumberland Beggar**

I recently turned fifty, which is young for
a tree, mid-life for an elephant and ancient
for a quarter-miler, whose son now says, 'Dad,
I just can't run the quarter with you any
more unless I bring something to read.'
Bill Cosby, **Time Flies**

But her father smiled on the fairest child
He ever held in his arms.
Emily Brontë, **A Day Dream**

To be a successful father ... there's one
absolute rule: when you have a kid, don't
look at it for the first two years.

Ernest Hemingway, **Papa Hemingway**

'Please don't pester me with so many questions.
I've answered you about a hundred times today
already. What do think would have happened if
I had asked my father so many questions?'
'Well Dad,' replied the boy. 'Perhaps you might
have learnt to answer some of mine.'

Ernest Hemingway, **Father to Son**

'Dad. Now that I'm 14 can I wear
silk stockings and a brassiere?'
'No, Derek, you can't!'

As you can see, I haven't quite got the hang of my new camcorder yet...

See how the kid's are getting on in the bath, dear...

Father to small boy: 'How many millions of times have I told you not to exaggerate?'

I used to tell a joke about the shame we suffered in Glasgow because he was a teetotaller, and the disgrace on Saturday nights of him being thrown into pubs.

Arnold Brown, **No Accounting for Comedy**

My father was the only person I ever knew who addressed babies in their prams as if they were his contemporaries. He spoke as he would to a bank manager or a bishop: friendly but respectful.

Joyce Grenfell, **George – don't do that**

Heredity is what a man believes in until
his son begins to behave like a delinquent.
Presbyterian Life

When I was a boy of fourteen, my father was
so ignorant I could hardly stand to have the
old man around. But when I got to be
twenty-one, I was astounded at how much
the old man had learned in seven years.
Mark Twain

Dad, Dad, when you come up to give
us a bit of real trouble, can you bring
us up a drink of water as well?
Michael Rosen, **These Two Children**

What did I tell you – he prefers the wrapping paper!

Calm down dear – I'm sure he didn't mean to stuff his sandwich into the video!

Now here's one - This man gets a telegram and he says, 'I'm happy today. I'm a daddy. I'm a daddy - after eighteen years I'm a daddy. And before the happy event my wife went to see a fortune-teller. The fortune-teller told her, "If it's a boy the father will die. If it's a girl the mother will die." I've got a letter here from me mother-in-law on me father's side. I'll read it to you - from me mother-in-law. It says:

"Your wife has presented you with a bouncing baby boy. Both doing well."

That'll tell you what the fortune-teller knows. Here I am, strong as a lion, game for anything. She goes on to say:

"PS - Sorry to say the milkman dropped dead this morning."'

Max Miller, **The Max Miller Blue Book**

Insanity is hereditary; you can
get it from your children.

Sam Levenson

My father could never have run a
filling station. Giving free air, or even
directions, would have left him apoplectic.

Richard Armour, **Pills, Potions - and Granny**

A father had invited a business friend to
lunch and when the joint was put on the
table, the young son of the house
exclaimed: 'Why, it's roast beef.'
'What did you expect then?' asked his mother.
'Well,' replied the boy, 'I heard Daddy
say last night that he was bringing a proper
mutton head home for lunch today.'

The one thing father always gave up
in Lent was going to church.
Clarence Day, **My Father's Dark Hour**

My father had a profound influence
over me - he was a lunatic.
Spike Milligan

If I had to say what I thought was one
of the most important things about
being a dad, it is 'being around'.
Michael Rosen, **Goodies and Daddies**

My father is in a bad mood.
This means he is feeling better.
Sue Townsend, **The Secret Diary of Adrian Mole**

Like father like son.

Proverb

My father told me everything about the birds and the bees. He doesn't know anything about girls!

Leopold Fechtner

Proud father: 'Our household represents the whole United Kingdom. I am English, my wife's Irish, the nurse comes from Scotland, and the baby wails.'

Did you hear about the wife who shot her husband with a bow and arrow because she didn't want to wake the children?

Leopold Fechtner

Charles reckons his school days were the best years of his life.

It is a wise father that knows his own child.
*William Shakespeare, **The Merchant of Venice***

I sometimes wished he would realise that he
was poor instead of being that most nerve-racking
of phenomena, a rich man without money.
*Peter Ustinov, **Dear Me***

I suppose that the high-water mark
of my youth in Columbus, Ohio, was
the night the bed fell on my father.
*James Thurber, **My Life and Hard Times***

Fatherhood is ...
pretending that the present you
love most is soap-on-a-rope.
Bill Cosby

We call him 'Rover.'
My husband wanted a dog.

I'll buy two – my wife's just had twins...

You are old Father William, the young man cried,
The few looks which are left you are grey;
You are hale, Father William, a hearty old man,
Now tell me the reason, I pray.
*Robert Southey, **The Old Man's Comforts,
and how he gained them***

The fundamental defect of fathers,
in our competitive society, is that they
want their children to be a credit to them.
*Bertrand Russell, **Sceptical Essays***

By the time a couple can really afford to
have children, they're having grandchildren.
Leopold Fechtner

You may go into the fields or down the
lane, but don't go into Mr McGregor's garden:
your Father had an accident there; he was put
in a pie by Mrs McGregor.
*Beatrix Potter, **The Tale of Peter Rabbit***

My Dad is brilliant ...
It's great to have a dad like mine. It's brilliant.
*Nick Butterworth, **My Dad is Brilliant***

Everyone grumbled. The sky was gray.
We had nothing to do and nothing to say.
... Then Daddy fell into the pond!
Alfred Noyes

A father's role at parties is to eat lots of ice cream.
*Michael Rosen, **Goodies and Daddies***

He's been trying to keep up with the younger generation for the last 30 years.

How's his piano practice coming on..?

He who teaches his son to swim at the top
of the waterfall will not long be a father.
Not the Nine O'Clock News, *1983*

A mother's pride, a father's joy!
Sir Walter Scott

New man: one who has read enough
babycare books to annoy women by telling
them what they are doing wrong.
Mike Barfield, **Dictionary for our Time**

The most important thing a father can do for his
children is to love their mother.
Theodore M. Hesburgh

Call not that man wretched who, whatever
ills he suffers, has a child to love.

Robert Southey

Oh tangled web do parents weave
When they think that their children are naive.

Ogden Nash

Children's children are the crown of old men;
And the glory of children are their fathers.

Proverbs, XVII:6

There are times when parenthood seems nothing
but feeding the mouth that bites you.

Peter De Vries

I told you dad – you're overweight!

She cut her first tooth today...

Dad is the dancing-man
The laughing-bear, the prickle-chin,
The tickle-fingers, jungle-roars,
Bucking bronco, rocking-horse,
The helicopter roundabout
The beat-the-wind at swing-and-shout
Goal-post, scarey-ghost,
Climbing-jack, humpty-back.

But sometimes he's
A go-away-please!
A snorey-snarl, a sprawly slump
A yawny mouth, a sleepy lump,

And I'm a kite without a string
Waiting for Dad to dance again.
Berlie Doherty, **Dad**

Father: A quarter-master and emissary
of subsistence provided by nature for
our maintenance in the period before
we have learned to live by prey.
Ambrose Bierce, **The Devil's Dictionary**

Being a father
Is quite a bother,
But I like it, rather.
Ogden Nash, **Soliloquy In Circles**

Children are a great comfort in your
old age - and they help you reach it faster, too.
Lionel Kaufman

*Isn't he getting a bit too old for all this
'baby on the lawn' stuff..?*

I said no more telly – it's bed time!

The fact that boys are allowed to exist at
all is evidence of a remarkable Christian
forbearance among men.

Ambrose Bierce

You're a kind of father figure to me, Dad.

Alan Coren

More boys would follow in their father's footsteps
if they weren't afraid of getting caught.

E.C. McKenzie

The worst misfortune that can happen to an
ordinary man is to have an extraordinary father.

Austin O'Malley

I don't think daddy will really appreciate your game of 'channel tunnels,' dear...

It is a wise child that knows its own father.
*Oliver Goldsmith, **Mystery Revealed***

The fathers have eaten sour grapes,
and the children's teeth are set on edge.
Ezekiel, XVIII:2

Speak roughly to your little boy.
And beat him when he sneezes:
He only does it to annoy,
Because he knows it teases.
*Lewis Carroll, **Alice's Adventures in Wonderland***

The follies of the fathers are no
warning to the children.
*Bernard le Bovier de Fontenelle, **Dialogues des morts***

It is impossible to please all the
world and also one's father.
Jean de la Fontaine

The parent who could see his boy as
he really is, would shake his head and say:
'Willie is no good: I'll sell him.'
Stephen Butler Leacock, **The Lot of the Schoolmaster**

Children suck the mother when they are
young, and the father when they are grown.
John Ray, **English Proverbs**

No man is responsible for his father.
That is entirely his mother's affair.
Margaret Turnball

The young son of the house ran into
the room where his mother was sitting
and said, 'Come at once, there's a man in
the kitchen kissing the au pair girl.'
As his mother rose to look into the matter he
cried out gleefully: 'April Fool, it's only father!'

The thing that impresses me most about America
is the way parents obey their children.
Edward, Duke of Windsor

What was silent in the father speaks
in the son; and often I found the
son the unveiled secret of the father.
Friedrich Nietzsche, **Thus Spake Zarathustra**

You've been bouncing him on your knee again, haven't you..!

*Let's keep the window closed, dear.
Daddy's changing the wheel...*

Greatness of name; in the father, oftimes helps
not forth, but overwhelms the son: they stand too
near one another. The shadow kills the growth.

Ben Jonson, **Timber, or Discoveries**

A Father is a banker provided by nature.

Anonymous

The affection of a father and a son are different:
the father loves the person of the son, and
the son loves the memory of his father.

Anonymous, **Characters and Observations**

Every generation revolts against its fathers
and makes friends with its grandfathers.

Lewis Mumford, **The Brown Decades**

*I told you not to make your father laugh
so soon after his hernia operation...*

Made a little slip-up haven't we, nurse?

A man is so in the way in the house.
Mrs Gaskell, **Cranford**

Parents are the bones on which
children sharpen their teeth.
Peter Ustinov, **Dear Me**

If the man who turnips cries,
Cry not when his father dies,
'Tis proof that he had rather
Have a turnip than his father.
Dr Samuel Johnson

Qualis pater talis filius:
As is the father, so is the son.
Anonymous

Fathers should be neither seen nor heard.
That is the only proper basis for family life.
Oscar Wilde, **An Ideal Husband**

Men who are ashamed of the way
their fathers made their money
are never ashamed to spend it.
Reflections of A Bachelor

I was the same kind of father as
I was a harpist - I played by ear.
Harpo Marx, **Harpo Speaks!**

We think our fathers fools, so wise we grow;
Our wiser sons, no doubt, will think us so.
Alexander Pope, **Essay on Criticism**

Acknowledgements:

The Publishers wish to thank everyone who gave permission to reproduce the quotes in this book. Every effort has been made to contact the copyright holders, but in the event that an oversight has occurred, the publishers would be delighted to rectify any omissions in future editions of this book. *5,000 One- and Two-Line Jokes*, Leopold Fechtner, Thorson's, a division of HarperCollins; *The Huge Joke Book*, Goldstein, Jackson, Ford and Newman, Clarion Books; *Time Flies*, Bill Cosby, reprinted courtesy of Bantam Books, a division of Transworld; *These Two Children*, Michael Rosen, reprinted courtesy of John Murray (Publishers) Ltd; *The Max Miller Blue Book*, Max Miller, reprinted courtesy of the author's estate; *Goodies and Daddies*, Michael Rosen, reprinted courtesy of John Murray (Publishers) Ltd; *The Tale of Peter Rabbit*, Beatrix Potter, reprinted courtesy of Frederick Warne, a division of Penguin Books; *Daddy Fell Into the Pond*, Alfred Noyes, reprinted courtesy of John Murray (Publishers) Ltd; *Dad,* Berlie Doherty, from *Another First Poetry Book*, reprinted courtesy of Oxford University Press; Ogden Nash, reprinted courtesy of Curtis Brown.